THE
SERVANT
LEADERSHIP

SOLUTION IN CONFLICT
MANAGEMENT

PASTOR CECIL HOLLAWAY

The Servant Leadership
Trilogy Christian Publishers
A Wholly Owned Subsidiary of Trinity Broadcasting
Network
2442 Michelle Drive
Tustin, CA 92780

For information, address Trilogy Christian Publishing
Rights Department, 2442 Michelle Drive, Tustin, Ca
92780.
Trilogy Christian Publishing/ TBN and colophon are
trademarks of Trinity Broadcasting Network.
For information about special discounts for bulk purchases, please contact Trilogy Christian Publishing.
Manufactured in the United States of America
Trilogy Disclaimer: The views and content expressed in
this book are those of the author and may not necessarily
reflect the views and doctrine of Trilogy Christian Publishing or the Trinity Broadcasting Network.
10 9 8 7 6 5 4 3 2 1
Library of Congress Cataloging-in-Publication Data is
available.
ISBN: 979-8-88738-611-9
ISBN: 979-8-88738-612-6

Dedication

To my beloved wife, Stella, who passed away on January 25, 2022. Stella Mae was a woman of God, loving wife, wonderful mother, protective sister, magnificent grandmother, caring aunt, and a beautiful person. Stella Mae, these two words alone hold a lot of meaning. If you had known Stella Mae, you knew what she stood for.

She believed in God and took care of her family. Many knew her as a no-nonsense woman, but she was equally as loving and embracing. Her faithfulness was inspiring, and her presence was majestic. Faithful, loving, kind, forgiving all these encompass the adjective of Stella Mae.

Truthfully, words could never describe how strong this woman was. She truly was a virtuous woman. The memories she left behind are priceless and will forever remain. Stella Mae Hollaway is a great example of a "Servant Leadership" spirit.

Preface

Due to the recent political events in the 2016 race to the White House, our society has been truly amazed and perplexed in understanding the leadership phenomenon. Because leadership is by far the most influential component to organizational resilience, longevity, and brand recognition. Therefore, in understanding the leadership phenomenon in conflict management, at least twenty-five percent of leadership effectiveness in conflict management should be spent on Servant Leadership. This book will examine servant leadership as an emerging leadership approach that appears more relevant and timely in the present context than other value-laden leadership approaches.

Keywords: Leadership, conflict, conflict management, servant leadership.

Acknowledgements

This book is the result of my Christian walk with God of learning and development from many mentors, teachers, supporters, advisors, friends, and family, who invested their time, energy, and interest in my life. For this, I am eternally grateful.

To my family, for your unwavering support.

To the members of Pilgrim Missionary Baptist Church Inc. who allowed me the privilege of sharing and testing the ideas and principles in this book in our relationship over the years. Thank you.

Introduction

This book will examine "Servant Leadership" as an effective principle in handling conflict management. The purpose of this book is to demonstrate how servant leadership styles on two critical aspects: 'the prioritization of subordinates' and ethical behavior' (Ehrhart, 2004, p. 73). Thus, an exploration of both the content and context of the narratives will illustrate the extent to which servant leadership both influence and correct social behavior and by doing so, help to resolve conflict issues.

So, in order to understand this book will examine leadership case histories, and scholarly literature, both primary and secondary sources. Within these documents, this book will be focusing on the behavior and communication strategies and by doing so the information will demonstrate the reasoning, purpose, and method behind the use of servant leadership and their effect on conflict issues.

Thus, when researching the reasoning behind servant leadership, the information, will be interpreting aspects of leadership styles. What this show us is this interpretation, as well as the demonstration of the ways in which the narrative provide data, are applications of the servant leadership emphasis. This information will be using qualitative methodology which will include analyzing the leadership case studies and servant leadership style provided by leading scholars.

While this information methodology will include a discourse analysis as well as an interpretation of servant leadership style. The analysis will provide a foundation of understanding in servant leadership styles. This approach will allow the concept to explore the communication strategies within leadership culture, ultimately, will show how said strategies influence organizational conflict issues.

Table of Contents

Chapter 1

The Origin of Servant Leadership

The literature by Greenleaf (1997), defines clearly that servant leaders are leaders who put other people's needs, aspirations, and interest above their own. The servant leader's deliberate choice is to serve others. In fact, the servant leader's chief motive is to serve first, as opposed to lead (Greenleaf, 1977). Furthermore, servant leaders seek to transform their followers to "grow healthier, wiser, freer, more autonomous, and more likely themselves to become servants" (Greenleaf, 1977: 13-14).

As a result of, while working as an AT&T executive, Greenleaf (1977) conceptualized the notion of servant leadership and introduced it into the organizational context. Interestingly, his concept has to a certain extent, some similarities with Burn's (1978) transforming leadership. Greenleaf (1977:13) claimed that:

The servant leader is a servant *first*......It begins with the natural feeling that one wants to serve, to serve first. Then conscious choice brings one to aspire to lead.... The difference manifest itself in the care taken by the servant-first to make sure that other people's highest-priority needs are being served.

Similarly, Burns (1978: 20) asserted that: (Transforming) leadership occurs when one or more persons engage with others in such a way that leaders and followers raise one another to higher levels of motivation and morality.... But transforming leadership ultimately becomes *moral* in that it raises the level of human conduct and ethical aspiration of both leader and led, thus it has a transforming effect on both.

However, servant leadership differentiates from other leadership styles on two critical aspects: 'the prioritization of subordinates' and ethical behavior' (Ehrhart, 2004, p.73). So, in understanding the leadership phenomenon in conflict management that is why twenty-five percent leadership effectiveness in conflict management should be servant leadership, because of the 'prioritization of subordinates and ethical behavior' that will give an 'interest-based" solutions in dealing with organizational conflicts.

This is why servant leaders act in the best interest of the employee and prioritize their individual growth and development. These actions result in higher levels organizational commitment (e.g., Jaramillo et al. 2009b), greater commitment to the supervisor (e.g., Walumbwa, Hartnell, and Oke 2010), and lower turnover intention (e.g., Hunter et al. 2013).

However, as it will be later shown in this book, how, servant leadership also affects the organization through various processes involving ethics.

Chapter 2

Famous People who have Leadership Language Style

Yet, while the words of a politician during a campaign can tell us a great deal about that person, including the leadership style we might expect him or her to utilize once in office. Since leadership language is magnified during elections, the 2008 United States Presidential election campaign speeches presented opportunities for analysis of leadership style based on the language used. The results indicated Hillary Clinton used more transformational language than Barack Obama. However, Barack Obama used more passive language than Hillary Clinton (Rahim, n.d.).

According to Rahim, (n.d.), "for Hillary Clinton, transformational leadership language was positively correlated with campaign month, while transactional language was negatively correlated with campaign month. Overall, the difference in mean frequency percentages of foreign policy issues language by campaign month was significant."

However, authentic leaders acknowledge the ethical responsibilities of their roles, can recognize and evaluate ethical issues, and take moral actions that are thoroughly grounded in their beliefs and values. Nevertheless, when we look at Donald Trump in the context of authentic leadership, we can see some of those qualities (Sage, 2015). According to Sage (2015), "for example, authentic leaders are self- aware-"know thyself." A prerequisite for being an authentic leader is knowing your own strengths, limitation, and values. Knowing what you stand for and what you value is critical. Moreover, self-awareness is needed in order to develop the other components of authentic leadership."

An authentic leader also exhibits relational transparency- "be genuine." This involves being honest and straightforward in dealing with others. An authentic leader does not play games or have a hidden agenda. You know where you stand with an authentic leaders. We certainly know where we stand with Donald Trump. He doesn't shy away from telling us what he thinks (Sage, 2015).

Consequently, "The Donald" misses the mark on the other two attributes of an authentic leader, which are to have balanced processing – "be fair-minded" and an internalized more perspective- "do the right thing." An effective authentic leader solicits opposing viewpoints and consider all options before choosing a course of actions" (Sage, 2015).

However, Barack Obama, Hillary Clinton, and Donald

Trump demonstrates certain interesting leadership style such as authentic, transformational, and transactional leadership language styles. In the opinion of the writer, they should focus on the servant leadership style that focus on others instead of their own self-interest.

Chapter 3

Defining and Measuring Servant Leadership Behavior in Organizations Transformational Leadership

In this section, this research examines the similarities and differences between servant leadership and other contemporary leadership models, namely transformational, authentic, and servant leadership.

First, servant leaders are more likely than transformational leaders to demonstrate the natural inclination to serve marginalized people. Bass (1985) argued that transformation leaders seek to empower and elevate followers rather than keep followers weak and dependent; however, the effect of that increased motivation and commitment will not necessarily benefit followers, as 'there is nothing in the transformational leadership model that says leaders should serve followers for the good of follower' (Graham, 1991, p. 110).

Thus, on the other hand, similar to Burns's (1978) transforming leadership, servant leadership requires that leaders are more likely than transformational leaders to set the following priorities in their leadership focus: followers first, organizations second, their own needs last (Graham, 1991). Hence, the focus of servant leadership, first and foremost, is on individual followers, and takes precedence over organizational objectives.

Which meant that, the rationale behind this deliberate focus on followers is well summarized by Stone et al. (2004, p. 355) who asserted the 'organizational goals will be achieved on a long-term basis only by first facilitating the growth, development, and general well-being of the individuals who comprise the organization. Unlike transformational leadership whose primary concern is 'performance beyond expectations,' the sine qua non of servant leadership is followers' holistic moral and ethical development. In fact, from its earliest conceptualization, servant leadership has been considered a leadership approach that elevates leaders and followers both morally and ethically (Greenleaf, 1977).

Chapter 4

Authentic Leadership

According to Avolio and Gardner (2005), acknowledged that servant leadership share similar key characteristics with authentic leadership, in that both explicitly recognize the importance of positive moral perspective, self- awareness, self-regulation (i.e., authentic behavior) positive modeling, and focus on follower development for a leader to function effectively. Authentic leaders are defined as individuals who have a deep awareness of their own and others' values/perspectives and the context in which they operate, and are positive in their outlook (Avolio et al., 2004; Gardner et al., 2005). These perspectives align with the servant leadership philosophy, although Avolio and Gardner (2005) suggested that follower self-awareness and self-regulation are missing from servant leadership behavior. The authors argue that most importantly, they observe that servant leadership emphasizes a spiritual orientation, which is not strongly highlighted in the authentic leadership model. The authors also argue that spirituality is an important source of motivation for servant leaders.

In short, the authors believe that spirituality is one of the many dimensions of servant leadership, but there are other equally important dimensions such as self-sacrificial servanthood and moral values, which are not clearly articulated in Fry's (2003) model.

Chapter 5

Servant Leadership

This is why the authors thus far shown how the model of servant leadership they propose in this paper extends the transformational, authentic, and spiritual leadership models. Our holistic model of servant leadership incorporates follower-oriented, service, spiritual, and moral dimensions of leadership sorely needed in the organizational context (Bass, 2000, p.33).

According to Bass (2000), sentiment that the strength of the servant leadership movement and its many links to encouraging follower learning, growth, and autonomy, suggests that the untested theory will play a role in the future leadership of the learning organization (p. 33). Furthermore, Greenleaf (1977) initiated the movement of servant leadership in organization on the basis of his reading of Herman Hess's (1956) Journey to the East, in which the servant, Leo becomes the leader through his servanthood to a group of people on a spiritual pilgrimage. Leo's story illustrated that behind the seemingly absurd and irrational coexistence of servanthood and leadership, there emerges a profound sense of leadership that begins with the natural feeling that one wants to serve, to serve first. Then conscious choice brings one to aspire to lead (Greenleaf, 1977, p.13).

Chapter 6

Servant Leadership and Conflict Coaching

Thus, conflict theorist sees society as a dynamic entity constantly undergoing change as a result of competition over scarce resources. Competition over scarce resources is the center of all social relationships. Conflict theorists believes competition, rather than consensus, is characteristics of human relationships. A concept that says broader social and the inherent competition entails; some people and organization have more resources (i.e., power, influence, culture, and leadership), and use those resources to maintain their posture of authority in society.

However, sociologists who work from the conflict perspective study the distribution or resources, power, and inequality. Sociologists when studying a social institution or phenomenon, they ask, "who benefits from this element of society?" According to the conflict perspective, inequalities in power and reward are built into all social structures. For example, in the United States, the dominant society constantly fight to maintain their privileged access to higher education by opposing measures that would broaden access, such as affirmative action or public funding. So, conflict coaching should be used under culture, leadership, and influences conflict situations.

According to Winslade and Pangborn (2015), conflict coaching is a relatively new concept, derived from the domain of executive coaching. Conflict coaching refers to conversations with one party to a conflict that do not reach the point of becoming a joint mediation. "Conflict coaching is a process in which a coach and client communication one-on-one for the purpose of developing the client's conflict-related understanding, interaction strategies, and interaction skills" (Jones and Brinkert, 2008, p.4). The concept of coaching has many meanings and is used in a variety of contexts. "In the ADR field, some practitioners used coaching to describe the interactions with parties during caucuses and premeditation and the assistance provided by mentors during mediation training. These are certainly forms of coaching, but an overview of the coaching field itself will provide a larger context to describe the growth and trends of conflict management coaching" (Brubaker, Noble, Fincher, Park & Press, 2014, p.359).

So, conflict coaching is an important concept to be use in conflict situations. Conflict is expensive to organizations. It produces low morale and work productivity, stress, sickness, high absenteeism rate, legal ramifications due to unnecessary disputes and so on, all contribute to workplace that produces destructive interaction. Besides the negative impact these situations have on the organizations, they reflect poorly on the organization and on leaders influences whose responsibilities include managing conflict. Research says the many organizations tend to react to conflict cultures, rather than consider preventative measures and other ways to move their culture to be conflict managed. In this regard, conflict coaching is emerging as a viable and proactive tool of choice. Conflict coaching should be use in cultural, leadership, and influence conflict situations.

While the leader has the potential to create the setting that becomes a powerful source of identification and commitment for employees (Schein, 1992). According to Denison (1990), " a few examples of coaching leaders to promote culture change include: (1) enhancing employees commitment and involvement in a company with an increasingly challenging marketplace; (2) anticipating problems from integrating two companies with differing cultures, and planning strategies to address conflict and competition for control; (3) assisting a new CEO to define his or her vision for the company when the former CEO and founder departs; and (4) increasing employee focus throughout on profitability, efficiency, and collaboration. In other words, executive coaching can play a powerful role in changing organizational culture. Finding executive coaches, like industrial and organization psychologists, who are both interpersonally effective and also are trained and experienced group dynamics, leadership development, and program design for assessing and measuring both individuals (e.g., attitudes, motivation) and business organizations (e.g., results, culture, climate) is particularly important to ensure there is a link between coaching activities and organizational outcomes.

Moreover, individual leadership resilience and growth process are all crucial parts of an effective coaching paradigm. Resilience has grown as a topic of interest to coaches and increases in resilience as a result of specific coaching programs are often reported (Grant, Curtayne, and Burton, 2009). However, the perspective of the coached leaders has remained largely unexplored. Leader often came to coaching as the result of facing a challenge and experienced significant experiential learning in relation to their resilience as a byproduct of coaching.

According to Smith (2015), a study was done to gain the leadership perspective on two key areas. Firstly, to assess if existing coaching might already be affecting resilience, despite that not being a contracted objective. Secondly, to identify what aspects of coaching might be most influential in leadership resilience" (p.6). Interview data was gathered from eight senior managers who had previous had coaching. Analysis was based on the grounded theory coding approach using NVivo software. All respondents reported that they felt coaching had enhanced their perceived resilience. Five overarching themes emerged that described how participants felt this was achieved:

1. Reclaim my self-belief

2. Learning

3. Seeing wider perspective

4. Supportive relationship

5. Thinking space

In analyzing these emergent five themes there was significant interaction and overlap between them (Smith, 2015, pgs. 6-10).

However, the results indicated that leaders did perceive coaching to have affected their resilience, even if this was not a defined objective for the coaching. In addition, leaders reported that coaching helped in five ways. It helped them reclaim their self-belief, it contributed to their learning, it helped them see the wider perspective, it provided a supportive relationship and gave them a thinking space" (Smith, 2015, p.6)

According to Smith (2015), leaders reported a clear perception that coaching they had received had helped their resilience. Participants in this study often brought current challenges to coaching and by working with these seemed to experience an increase in resilience as a byproduct of their coaching. Coaches, therefore, need to be aware that their coaching may already be affecting resilience, but also that when resilience is under threat, they may already be affecting resilience, but also that when resilience is under threat, they may need to adapt their coaching style to support resilience overtly. However, the findings also highlight the importance of a supportive relationship during times of challenge and that just learning about tools and cognitive strategies alone may not be adequate. Leaders often came to coaching as a result of facing challenge but did not contract for resilience outcomes specifically. They were frequently experiencing a loss of confidence and an inability to step back and take a wider perspective on the situation. Coaches might, therefore, consider the following as key steps to consider when working with leaders in the resilience domain:

1. **Self-belief-** Even leaders who are very senior and may have previously demonstrated exceptional confidence may need interventions to re-build self-confidence. The level of challenge may need

to be reduced with a higher focus on validation and support.

2. **Learning- Maintaining** a focus on learning by directing attention to create holistic learning about self, others, and personal strategies may prove more valuable that just teaching cognitive strategies. While tools and techniques might prove useful, personal learning seems more valuable.

3. **Seeing the wider perspective-** It appears that pressure can narrow the focus of attention for individuals so continued attention to the wider system, other potential points of view and alternative perspective can be helpful.

4. **Supportive relationship-** Highlighting the independence and neutrality of the coaching space and allowing emotional expression may reduce the resources occupied in the suppression of feelings. This may give benefits through the release of energy.

5. **Thinking space-** Maintaining and protecting the private thinking space that focuses on personal needs rather than just problem solving is important. While leaders are busy and are often overly focused on the needs of others and taking action,

they need to understand the benefit of the personal reflective space that coaching can provide. While counterintuitive this 'time-out' may ultimately provide a solution that might never have emerged from endless rumination and analysis" (p. 18).

However, servant leadership gives emphasis to the needs to the follower over the self-interests of the leaders (Laub, 1999) and characterize the leader's behavior as servant first (Greenleaf, 1977). The servant leader seeks to meet the needs of the follower through actions that empower the follower by the sharing of power and a practice of authenticity in leadership that favors the follower (Laub, 1999). The coach, as servant leader, works with his or her client to aid in the discovery of the foundational values of what truly motivates them. The coach analyzes this information to develop a framework that will help him or her work effectively with the client to achieve the desired results (Gladis, 2007, p. 61). The coach understands that the key to maximizing the performance of the client is to unlock and strengthen the client's potential (Whitmore, 1996). The servant coach provides help and support for his or her client that is systemic and desirably perpetual throughout the duration of the client's career that is personalized, beneficial, and maximizes the client's potential (CIPD, 2007).

Chapter 7

Servant Leadership and Negotiation

THE CASE OF THE TWELVE ANGRY MEN:

The parties involved

This case study is about twelve male jurors confined to a jury room to decide the guilt or innocence of a young Hispanic boy in a murder trial. Before sending the twelve jurors to make this decision, the judge reminds them that their verdict must be unanimous and that if they hold "reasonable doubt" as to the guilt of the young boy then their verdict must be "not guilty." If however, they find the young boy guilty then he will be sentenced to death. Each juror's obligation is to fulfill his civic duty and to be ruled of his own conscience (*Twelve Angry Men*.www.youtube.com).

The negotiation styles

In the negotiation environment it is structured by the relationship between the jurors, and the resources and constraints within the environment, and the bargaining power. In other words, how much bargaining power each jurors has to influence each other and can it, changes the elements of the negotiation (*Twelve Angry Men*, www.youtube.com). "Power, like other negotiation conditions, is in this sense in the eyes of the beholder" (Reardon, 2005, pg.11). Once you believe that power is yours, it shows.

The relationship dynamics

In this case, the jurors have no existing relationships with each other prior to the case and are not expected to form any relationship after the trial. Therefore, this jury should have less competitive behavior because they are not expected to maintain any outside relationship. Furthermore, no teams exist; each juror is responsible to himself and to the law. So, the jurors should only make a conscience and legal decision.

The resources and constraints

Which means that, the jurors' resources and the constraints on their decision appear to be limited because they have no access to the outside world and have no means to ask for further evidence or even leave the room to which they are confined. But because of the tactics of Juror 8 uses, the resources and constraints seem to change quite often. According to Reardon (2005), "For a negotiator to achieve versatility requires a clear understanding of the primary obstacles to successful negotiation inquiry-faulty assumption" (pg. 7). The resources the jury had were the evidence and the witness and argument made by the prosecutor and the defense attorney. The internal constraints the jury had were time to make a decision so that they can return back to the lives and being confined to a lock room. The external constraints the jury had were the law and to deliver justice (*Twelve Angry Men*, www.youtube.com).

The bargaining objectives and issues (interests)

Which resulted in some of the bargaining objectives the jurors had were to punish the defendant. **Juror 8** wanted to consider the possibility of innocence. **Juror 11** had blind faith in the American system and success of democracy and justice. **Juror 10** had racist convictions against the defendant and wanted to suppress the minorities. **Juror 7,** wanted to finish quickly to go to a baseball game. **Juror 3** was hostile toward the accused because of his failed relationship with his son. **Juror 8** however, seems to understand that bargaining power is both relative and subjective because it is based on the party's perception of each other (*Twelve Angry Men*, www.tube.com).

The Best Alternative to a Negotiated Agreement (BATNA)

However, the best alternative to a negotiated agreement is should the jurors failed to reach a unanimous verdict they can walk out and declare a "hung jury," which would result in a mistrial.

The issue of social influence and persuasion

In this case study, the issues of social influence and persuasion, Juror 8 was a masterful negotiator. He skillfully used several negotiation techniques. He builds alliances, uses brainstorming, offers concessions, anticipates offers, and reframes and masters the factual information. He encourages engagement and uses the strengths and weaknesses of his counterparts to his advantage. Juror 8 manipulates the rules of the game and the resources and relationship available in order to build a base for action and establish himself as the leader of the negotiation. This exemplary of negotiation proclaim a "not guilty" verdict. According to Reardon (2005), "Many negotiations fail before they get off the ground because of style differences. One thing a negotiator never wants to be is predictable" (pg. 47).

In the opinion of the writer, Juror 8 demonstrated the principles of the servant leader by putting the defendant interest before the interests of the other jurors.

Chapter 9

Servant Leadership and Organizational Systems Analysis and Design

Because trust allows people to believe in the honesty, integrity, reliability, and justice of those with whom they interact. Changes in trust are usually driven by reciprocity: the idea that if one person does something for or to another, the other will respond in a similar manner (Blackard and Gibson, 2002). Policies intended to ensure workplace effectiveness, justice, fairness, and peace often instead cause significant counterproductive conflict. Conflict resulting from policies can be direct, as between employees and the organization represented by the policy; or secondary, where they provide an incentive for unacceptable employee behavior or conflict among employees. Management cannot prevent all policy-based conflict. It can, however, do a number of things to reduce its amount and severity. These include the following:

- Not promulgate unneeded policies
- Derive its policies from core values

- Consider the systems implications of policy

- Involve employees in policy implementation

- Effectively communicate policies

- Provide fair administration

- Build dispute resolution processes into policies

- Update policies to keep up with changing times (Blackard and Gibson, 2002).

However, resistance to management-initiated change is a frequent cause of organizational conflict. Change is the process of moving from the status quo, through a transition, to another status quo. Targets of change go through predictable phases in adjusting to change they perceive as negative. Resistance to change and consequent conflict may be passive and unseen or active and confrontational. It may occur for many reasons. All resistance to change cannot and should not be avoided. Instead, management should minimize, rather than try to overcome, resistance through actions such as the following:

- Don't surprise employees

- Give employees a voice

- Communicate changes effectively

- Ensure effective supervisor-subordinate relationships

- Provide an outlet for the conflict that does develop

- Deal effectively with conflict that is surfaced (Blackard and Gibson, 2002).

This is why servant leadership theory brings out the importance of trust in social, economic, and political organization is considered significantly. Therefore, the leader's behavior is thus more important than that anyone else in determine the level of trust that exists within a group or organization (Aryee, Budhwar, and Chen, 2002). Trust between management and employees will have a large impact on the quality of public management. Thus, the shortage of trust in public organization is one the main factors lead to uninventive and indifferent employees. It seems that the servant leadership is an appropriate solution to address this problem in the government agencies because trust is one of the indicators of servant leadership (Dennis, 2004). In fact, the servant leadership have been supported and implemented in some of the most successful American companies (Sendjaya, and Sarros, 2002).

However, honesty and integrity are essential factors a good leader, based on the history of leadership. These values can cause the creation of people trust and organizational trust. Leaders who have honesty can inspiration trust to other (Liden, Wayan, Zhoa, and Henderson, 2005). Thus, the servant leadership model is not described the organization members who have less abilities compare to his manager, but also give competence to employees such as managers of the organization. All members have equal dignity and all of them are active and participate in management decisions. Greenleaf believes that servant leadership is based on service philosophy and the servant leadership prefer the empowerment, trust, cooperation, ethical use of power and serve to others rather than other things (Lee, 2004).

So, if we believe that the servant leadership is differing form other style there, we should introduced from other style therefore, and we should introduced different dimensions for it (Bennis and Nanus, 1997).

After reading numerous articles and reviews, ten features for servant leaders that are enumerated:

- Listening
- Empathy
- Healing
- Awareness
- Persuasion
- Conceptualization

- Foresight

- Stewardship

- Commitment to the growth of people

- Building community (Laub, 1999).

According to Hamilton (2008), several positive outcomes can be observed at servant-led organizations, including the following:

- Mission and value focus;

- Creativity and innovation;

- Responsiveness and flexibility;

- Commitment to both internal and external service;

- Respect for employees; employee loyalty; and

- Celebration of diversity (pp. 77-78).

There is, however, no empirical evidence to support these assumptions. Joseph and Winston (2005, p.16), "have also claimed that servant-leadership has the potential to improve an organization's productivity and financial performance; however, they cite references that lack any empirical evidence to support their claim (Andersen, 2009).

Research Design and Recommendations

This research study used Barbuto and Wheeler's (2006) Servant Leader Questionnaire to assess mid-level service managers of three high-performing automobile dealership to determine whether they were considered by their employees to exhibit servant-leader behaviors. This is one of few empirical studies of this model in the for-profit market. The study also measured demographic variables (gender, age, education, and length of service) to determine whether perceptions of the manager were affected by any of these factors.

A. Subjects

Subjects were mid-level managers and their employees at three automobile dealerships identified by their manufactures as high performing in their region and dealership size.

B. Interviews

Qualitative interviews were conducted a priori in order to determine whether there were main themes that reflected the senior leader's "servant leader" orientation. Questions were developed based on the servant leader's literature to extract response that would provide in-depth knowledge of the leaders' interaction with their employees. Examples of questions are "Who is your role model for your leadership style?" "How is training done?" "What tools and help do the employee need?" Because the interviews revealed behaviors and attitudes consistent with servant leadership, it was deemed appropriate to proceed with the distribution of the Servant Leader Questionnaire (Barbuto and Wheeler, 2006).

C. Surveys

Each employee received the appropriate version(s) of the questionnaire which were distributed by the investigators to ensure a complete sample. Each questionnaire packet included a consent form as well as a postage-paid envelope addressed to the investigators.

V. Results

According to Melchar and Bosco, (2010), "our results support the contention that the modeling of servant leadership by strategic level managers can create an organizational culture in which servant leaders develop among lower-level managers. Servant leadership can provide a successful alternative to other leadership styles such as autocratic, performance-maintenance, transactional, or transformational. Servant leadership has been effective within the three companies that participated in this study. The top service ratings at each of these companies add to increased business through customer loyalty. No significant differences were noted in the perceptions of the leadership style of the managers based on employee age, length of time with the company, or level of education... These results suggest that servant leadership should be effective for most, if not all, employees (p. 84).

According to Melchar and Bosco, (2010), "We were able to empirically test the servant-leader model in three high-performing organizations whose employees are expected to perform their duties at a very high level. This was a unique opportunity to examine the theory in a non-laboratory setting. There were limitations, however, in that we did examine only one industry. Therefore, our results may not be generalizable to other types of for-profit environments. In addition, our sample size was somewhat small, although the coefficient alphas were consistent with those in the Barbuto and Wheeler (2006) study" (p. 85).

Conclusion

Furthermore, since most of the leading theorists and researchers introduced servant leadership theory as a valid model for the modern organization. "However, this leadership style is not yet supported by empirical research" (Fridell, Belcher, Messner, 2009). "But the concept of servant leadership has this potential that can change organizations and communities. Because servant leadership can design organizational and personal change. In this method, all members of the organization have same rights, similar information, and same vision and the leadership role is facilitating the formation of the group in organization. This leadership style can help organization in today's world because it has various concepts and has ability to strengthen the sympathy in the organization. Trust is one of the concepts that will effect the relationship between leader and follower. Leaders who are trusted by their followers can easily make sense of commitment and responsibility in their followers.

What this shows us is that trust to leaders can affect many results of organization and based on many research trust in one of the main dimensions of servant leadership.

So, the servant leadership style can be a good mechanism for building trust in the organization" (Laub, 1999; Nyhan, 2000; Sendjaya, Sarros, 2002).

"This research shows that there is as relationship between servant leadership and organizational trust and with entire the leader trust and organizational communication as moderator the intensity of this relationship was increased. This finding is related to previous studies provide evidence of relationship between servant leadership and organizational trust due attention to leader trust and organizational communication" (Joseph, & Winston, 2005). So that is why twenty-five percent of leadership effectiveness in conflict management should be spent on servant leadership.

References

Andersen, J. A. (2009). "When a Servant-leader Comes Knocking . . ." *Leadership & Organization Development Journal,* 30: 4-15

Aryee, S.; Budhwar, p.s.; Chen, Z., X. (2002), "Trust as a mediator of the relationship between organizational justice and work outcomes: test of a social exchange model, Journal of organizational Behavior, No. 23, pp. 267-285.

Avolio, G. J., Gardiner, W. L., Walumbwa, F. O., Luthans, F. and May, D. R. (2004). "Unlocking the mask: a look at the process by which authentic leaders' impact follower attitudes and behaviors". *Leadership Quarterly,* 15, 801-823.

Avolio, B. J. and Gardner, W. L. (2005), "Authentic leadership development: getting to the root of positive forms of leadership." *Leadership Quarterly,* **16.** 315-338.

Barbuto, J. E., and D. W. Wheeler (2006). "Scale Development and Construct Clarification of Servant Leadership." *Group & Organization Management, 31* (3): 300-326

Bass, B. M. (1985). *Leadership and Performance Beyond Expectations*. New York: Free Press.

Bass, B. M. (2000). "The Future of Leadership in Learning Organizations" *Journal of leadership Studies*, 7, 18-40

Bennis, W.: Nanus, B. (1997) "Leaders: strategies for taking charge" New York: Harper Collins publishers.

Blackard, K. and Gibson, J. W. (2002). *Capitalizing On Conflict: Strategies and Practices for Turning Conflict to Synergy in Organizations: A Manager's Handbook.* (1st Ed). Palo Alto: Davies-Black Publishing

Burns, J. M. (1978). *Leadership*. New York: Harper & Row.

CIPD. (2007). *Coaching in Organizations*. London: The Chartered Institute of Personnel and Development (CIPD).

References

Denison, D. R. (1990). *Corporate Culture and Organizational Effectiveness.* Wiley.

Dennis, R. S. (2004), "Servant leadership theory: Development of the servant leadership theory assessment instrument" A Dissertation presented for the degree Doctor of philosophy.

Ehrhart, Mark. G. (2004). "Leadership and Procedural Justice Climate as Antecedents of Unit-level Organizational Citizenship Behavior." *Personnel Psychology 57*(1): 61-94, DOI: 10.1111/j.1744-6570.2004.tb02484.x.

Earley, P. C., and Ang, S. (2003). Cultural intelligence: Individual interactions across culture.

Explorations in Theory and Practice, *2*(1), pp. 90-118. Retrieved from: http://journals.gmu.edu/NandC/issue/2

Fridell, M.; R. N.; Messener, P. E. (2009), "Discriminate analysis is gender public school principal servant leadership differences" Leadership & Organizational Development Journal, Vol. *30,* No. 8, pp 722-763.

Galpin, T.J. and Herndon, M. (2000). The complete guide to mergers and acquisitions: Process

Grant, A. (2006). Evidence based coaching handbook. (1st Ed.). Hoboken, NJ:

Gardner, W. L., Avolio, B. J., Luthans, F., May, D. R. and Walumbwa, F. O. (2005). "Can you see the real me?" A self-based model of authentic leader and follower development. *Leadership Quarterly*, **16**, 343-372.

Graham, J. W. (1991). 'Servant-leadership in organizations: inspirational and moral' *Leadership Quarterly*, **2**, 105-119.

Grant, A., Curtayne, L., and Burton, G. (2009). Executive coaching enhances goal attainment,

Gladis, S. (2007). Executive coaching building steam in organizations. T+D, *61* (12), 59-6.

Greenleaf, A., R. K. (1977). *Servant leadership: A journey into the nature of legitimate power and greatness.* New York: Paulist Press.

Hamilton, F. (2008). "Servant Leadership." In Leadership: The Key Concepts, eds. A.

Marturano and J. Gosling, 146-150, London: Routledge.

Hesse, H. (1956). *Journey to the East.* London: Owen.

Hunter, Emily M., Mitchell J. Neubert, Sara, Jansen Perry, L. A. Witt, Lisa M. Penney, and Evan

Hofstede, G. (1997). *Cultures and organization: Software of the mind.* New York: McGraw-Hill http://mediate.com/articles/noble3.cfm International Coaching Psychology Review, *10*(1). Retrieved from Ebscohost John Wiley & Sons.

Jaramillo, Fernando, Douglas B. Grisaffe, Lawrence B. Chonko, and James A.Roberts. (2009b). "Examing the Impact of Servant Leadership on Salesperson's Turnover Intention." Journal of Personal Selling& Sales Management *29*(4): 351-365. DOI: 10.2753/PSSO885-3131290404.

Jones, T. and Brinkert, R. (2008). Conflict coaching: Conflict management strategies and skills

Joseph, E.; Winston, B. (2005), A correlation of servant leadership, leader trust and organization trust," Leadership & Organizational Development Journal Vol. *26,* No. 1, pp. 6-22.

Laub, J. A. (1999), "Assessing the servant organization: development of the servant organizational leadership Assessment (SOLA) instrument" unpublished doctoral dissertation, Florid Atlantic University, Boca Raton.

Lee, H. J. (2004), "The role of competence-based trust and organizational identification in continues improvement" Journal of Managerial Psychology, Vol *19*, No. pp. 623-639.

Liden, R. C.; Wayan, S. J.; Zhoa, H.: Henderson, D. (2005), "Development of multidimensional measure of servant leadership" Management association, Charleston, SC.

Noble. C. (2003). Conflict Coaching for Leaders. Retrieved from resilience and workplace well-being: A randomized controlled study, The Journal of Positive Psychology, *4*(5), 396-407. Retrieved from Ebscohost

Nyhan, R. C. (2000), "Changing the paradigm: trust and its role in public sector an organizations" American Review of public Administration Vol. *30*, No.1. pp. 87-109.

Rahim. M. A. (n.d.). Managing Diverse Situations in Organizations. Current Topics in Management, Vol 15, 2011, pp.1-9.

Reardon, K. (2005). *Becoming A Skilled Negotiator* (1st ed). New Jersey: John Wiley and Sons.

Rosinski. P., and Abbott. N. G., (2006). *Coaching from a Cultural Perspective*.

Schein, E. (1992). *Organizational culture and leadership*. Jossey-Bass.

Sage. E. (2015). "Is Donald Trump an Authentic Leader?" Retrieved from http://www.ethicssage. com/2015/091is-donald-trump-an-authentic-leader-.html

Sendjaya, S.; Sarros, J. C. (2002). "Servant leadership: its origin, development, and application in organizations" Journal of leadership and organizational studies, Vol. *9*, No.2, pp.57-64.

Smith, L.C. *How coaching helps leadership resilience: The Leadership perspective*, 2015. https://doi. org/10.1002/erq.21104. Stone, A. G., Russell, R. F. and Patterson, K. (2004). 'Transformational versus servant leadership: a difference in leader focus. *Leadership & Organization Development Journal*, 25, 349-361.

12 Angry Men. United States: United Artists Corp., 1957.

Walumbwa, Fred O., Chad A. Hartnell, and Adegoke Oke. (2010). "Servant Leadership, Procedural Justice Climate, Service Climate, Employee Attitudes, and Organizational Citizenship Behavior: A Cross-level Investigation." Journal of Applied Psychology *95*(3): 517-529. DOI: 10.1037/a0018867.

Weinberger. "Servant Leaders Inspire Servant Followers: Antecedents and Outcomes for Employees and the Organization ." Challenge validation, 2013. https://www.dnb.com/business-directory/company-profiles.sage_publications_inc.69ab28bb-1304bea50f0deb2986bce82e.html. The Leadership Quarterly 24(2):316-331. DOI: 10.1016/j.leaqua.2012.001 for the individual. Thousands Oaks, CA: Sage Publications. Retrieved from Ebscohost

Winslade, John, and Ashley Pangborn. "Narrative Conflict Coaching." *Narrative and Conflict: Explorations in Theory and Practice* 2, no. 1 (2015): 90. https://doi.org/10.13021/g8w88g.

About the Author

Pastor Cecil Hollaway
Pastor, Teacher

Pastor Cecil Hollaway: Pastor of Pilgrim Missionary Baptist Church Inc.

Pastor Hollaway is a native of Baltimore, Md. He was called into the teaching Ministry in 1989 by Our Lord and Savior Jesus Christ. The first Sermon he taught was from the Gospel of John 3rd chapter 16th verse.

He first worked as a youth Sunday school teacher at Calvary Baptist in Colorado Springs, CO. He later became an associate pastor and Sunday school superintendent at New Testament Church of God In Christ in Colorado Springs, CO. In 1991, he moved to Louisville, KY and was licensed as a minister at Pilgrim Missionary Baptist Church in Louisville, KY. In 1992, he later moved to Lexington, KY because of a great job opportunity there, whereby he was ordained on June 10, 1994, at New Hope Christian Inc. in Lexington, KY.

His first work as a pastor was in November 1995 where he was sent by Christ to Nicholasville, KY, to Refreshing

Ministries of Nicholasville, KY. He was ordained on June 23, 1996. Pastor Hollaway received his 3rd ordination on October 25, 1998, by Grace fellowship Ministries Inc. In 2006, he was then called to pastor Word of Life Fellowship in Louisville, KY.

In 2011, Pastor Hollaway was called to pastor, Pilgrim Missionary Baptist Church, Inc.

Pastor Hollaway's civic and social involvements have been speaker at the "Promise Keepers" ministries, a volunteer chaplain at the Jessamine Detention Center in Nicholasville, KY, a volunteer chaplain at Marion Adjustment Center (prison) in Lebanon, KY. He also received a volunteer appreciation award on April 14, 2002, from their organization.

In 2010, Pastor Hollaway earned his Bachelor of Science Degree in Paralegal Studies. In 2016, Pastor Hollaway earned his Master of Science Degree in Conflict Management and Leadership.

Pastor Cecil Hollaway was married to the late Evangelist Stella M. Hollaway. They have six grown children and twenty-five grandchildren and two great-grandchildren. Above all, Pastor Cecil Hollaway is just a down to earth, God-fearing man, teaching people about the Kingdom of God, leadership abilities.